For Alan

Happy Readin'

from the author

AB Charles

5/8/15

DRAGONS GUARD THE ZOO
ISBN 978-0-932529-69-5

Text © A. B. Curtiss 2010
Illustrations © A. B. Curtiss 2010

Cataloging-in-publishing data

Curtiss, Arline B.
        Dragons Guard the ZooA/B. Curtiss
        p.cm
        SUMMARY: Poetry and nursery rhymes
        ISBN 978-0-932529-69-5

        1. Juvenile fiction 2. Poetry-Fiction

        PZ8.3.C8785dr   2010

Printed in China.

Dragons
Guard the
ZOO

A. B. Curtiss

A Note from the Author

This book began in poems and songs I wrote to entertain my 5 children, then my 13 grandchildren. And to be truthful, to entertain myself as well.

My daughter's triplets, Reagan, McKay and Kelsey inspired *The Brave Little Triplets* part. I took care of them for the first three months of their lives. I couldn't hold them all at once when they were fussy, so I'd put them down on a blanket on the rug, pick up my guitar and sing to them, often making up songs as I went along. Then, when baby sister Delaney arrived, Grammy temporarily moved in again.

Some of the poems came at the request of the older grandchildren. They'd say, "Write a poem about being jealous of a kid at school," or "Do one about my cat."

I handcrafted a small book of these poems for my grand-daughter Harmony's 16th birthday. She took it to college, and so treasured the book, she has inspired me to offer the "family poetry book" for publication. Everybody has at least one poem with their name. Everybody includes my husband Ray; sons, Deane, Ford and Wolf; daughters, Sunday and Demming; sons-in-law, Kyle and Dave; daughters-in-law, Shelli and Paula; my grandchildren, Blueray and his new wife Teodora, Solmar, Harmony, Peregrine, Summer, Cutter, Tanner, Mavrik, Ayla, Reagan, McKay, Kelsey and Delaney.

And now the book is for you as well. I hope you will find the verses good company, and that you will also see yourself somewhere on these pages.

A. B. Curtiss

This book is dedicated
to my son, Wolf,
who, though very
observant,
is a man of few words.

This Book is for You

This book is for you,
You tellers of tales,
You riders of dragons,
You watchers of whales.
Open any page to begin,
And if you must leave
Then come back again.

When Lions Walk

When lions are walking
And taking some air,
It really is better
If you are not there.

Upside Down

Suppose the world went upside down
And things stopped being how they should.
Imagine circles turning square,
And shadows growing thick as wood.
Suppose the clouds dropped to the ground,
And every number was a word.
Imagine pictures painting artists,
Music, seen but never heard.
Suppose all creatures in the zoo
Began, instead, to be us?
When we were all in cages.
Would the animals come to see us?

Dragons Guard the Zoo

Dragons guard the zoo at night,
How fierce they fly through the air.
But the elephants seem to like them,
And so does the panda bear.
When all the cages are locked up tight,
And a hush comes over the grounds,
And there's not a single person in sight,
The dragons start making their rounds.
The koala bears hardly notice
When the dragons whirr overhead
With a low and a mournful whistling sound
As the zoo creatures scurry to bed.
Then all night long the dragons croon
Their stories and lullabies.
And all sleep safe under dragons' wings
That glide through the starry skies.

His Favorite Horse

I once knew a man so distinctly absurd
He claimed that his favorite horse was a bird.
There's no need to laugh,
I'm not pulling your leg.
When he stops for breakfast
His horse lays the egg.

Dave Saw a Bear

Dave saw a bear while hunting deer
And hoped it wouldn't mind him.
He zigged and zagged the whole way home
So that the bear couldn't find him.
Dave thought the bear was far away
But his shadow redefined him,
And there he stood all tooth and growl
As if Dave had maligned him.
The bear, thought Dave, can't reach the roof
If the ladder disinclined him.
But sad to say when Dave climbed up,
The bear was right behind him.

The Last Fight

One monster had a short, short snout,
One had a long, long nose.
They took a dislike to each other, so the story goes.
The short, short-snouted monster thought,
The world's not big enough
For me and him with that long nose
Who thinks that he's so tough.
If push would ever come to shove
I know that I could beat him.
Since food is getting rather scarce,
Perhaps it's time to eat him.
The monster with the long, long nose
Had a similar fate in mind
For his short, short-snouted neighbor
Whom he thought would taste just fine.
There wasn't any question
That the two were going to fight.
The day of battle finally dawned
On a deafening, fearsome sight!
The other animals scattered
As the bloody war began.
The monsters clawed and ripped and gnawed,
They shrieked, they fell, they ran.
They devoured one another
In a manner bold and deft,
For with each chew they smaller grew
Until neither one was left.

The Boy was Mean

The boy was mean to insects, the boy was mean to bugs.
He ripped the wings off flies, and stuck pins into slugs.
What do you think that boy would do
If insects weren't so small?
What do you think that boy would do
With a spider six feet tall?

A Giant Chicken

We met a giant chicken in the woods,
And hardly could believe our own eyes.
Why that chicken was three times our own size.
Since this was not the kind of hen we're used ter,
We did not wait around to meet a rooster.

The Cats Dreadful Duet

At the meeting two cats said they'd sing a duet
For a night's entertainment none soon would forget.
They started out loud, and in seconds were reaching
The top of their voices. The sound was so screeching,
Earsplitting, and piercing no one could believe it.
All covered their ears as they tried to relieve it.
The first verse was gruesome, by their second stanza
The crowd began moving out on the veranda
To try and escape the shrill voices, walls shaking,
The panes in the windows all cracking and breaking.
The pitchers of water and glasses all shattered,
But on the cats sang as if none of that mattered.
Meanwhile the firemen (may they save us from harm)
Mistook the high notes for a fire alarm.
So in they all rushed when the third verse had ended,
Spraying water on all, but none were offended.
The audience, happy to break up the meeting;
The two cats remarking they knew fame was fleeting.
In the months that ensued, the cats often vowed
They'd be happy to sing, once again, for the crowd.
They practiced their screeching, their howling, and humming,
But no invitation was ever forthcoming.

15

The Bees Nest

I should have left that bees nest where it hung.
I knocked it down and then, of course, got stung.
This is not an ordinary day
(That's because the bees got in my way).
And this is not an ordinary dance
(That's because the bees got in my pants).

The Crocodile.

A green crocodile swimming in the bayou
Called out to two rabbits, "May I invite you
To join me tonight for a bit of nice stew?"
The rabbits hopped off with a firm "No, thank you!"

The crocodile noticed two plump little fishes
And spoke to them softly, "Come here if you wishes
And we will partake of some very fine dishes."
"No thanks," they both murmured, becoming suspicious.

The crocodile then spied a little gray eel,
And he spoke with great charm, "You are hungry I feel,
Poor thing, let me make you a nutritious meal."
She demurred with a dread she could barely conceal.

The crocodile next heard a lonely goat bleat.
At last, he thought hungrily, now I will eat.
But the goat was no goat, and beat a retreat,
Thus saving himself from becoming dead-meat.

The Hippopotamus

Since it's larger than a lot of us
They named it hippopotamus.
It's the biggy of the piggy family.
He has a temper when he's riled,
He might look placid but he's wild.
When you see him in the Zoo
You seldom have so fine a swine,
So big a pig to view.

The Whale

An elephant came to the edge of the sea,
The creature he saw there looked smaller than he.
Quite rudely he called to the little black snout,
"How deep is the water? I'd like to wade out.
But you see I'm so large, begging your pardon,
A shrimp small as you would not have a problem
In this shallow pool. But perhaps out beyond
There runs deeper water in your little pond."
Then up thrust the whale with a gigantic bellow,
"Jump right in if you think you can swim, Little Fellow!"
The lesson is: Seeing's not always believing;
First appearances can be extremely deceiving.

Music Hath Charms

A fox once caught a bunch of frogs
To cook up for his party.
The frogs were plump and juicy,
His guests would all eat hearty.
But just before becoming soup,
One frog said, "Don't deny us.
We'd like to treat you to a song
Before you bake or fry us."
What a nice touch, thought the fox,
To entertain my guests.
And so the frogs began to croak,
Taking all requests.
Their tone was quite monotonous
And the guests were too polite
To interrupt the concert,
So the frogs droned on all night.
Before long, heads began to nod.
Eyelids were closing by the score.
When everybody fell asleep,
The frogs escaped with no encore.
The fox was mad the frogs deceived him
In the situation previous.
But, put someone in mortal fear,
And they're likely to turn devious.

It's Hard to Look Duck in the Eye

It's hard to look Duck in the eye
Now that Mother has made the dressing
That we'll have for Sunday dinner,
And *he'll* be what we'll be blessing.

The Long-Long-Necked Giraffe

The long-long-necked giraffe
Is an innocent looking creature.
With his knobby horns, and soulful eyes,
He hasn't a single feature,
From his funny ears to his spindly legs,
That looks like he'd mistreatchur.

The Nice Dog

The children called their mother,
"Look at this nice dog we found.
He likes to dance and chase around.
He makes a growling sound
But never barks at all,
And he comes when we call.
We gave him some water to drink.
He's a good old dog, don't you think?"

Their mother's face turned pale with fright,
Her eyes were in a stare.
The children thought they'd found a dog.
What did they find?
A BEAR!

Two Chickens

A rooster and a hen who lived deep in a swamp
Tried hard to keep their eggs from cooling in the damp.
That hen, she sat upon her eggs in a most devoted way.
And yet one time she found an egg she thought had rolled away.
That egg was so far from the nest, the hen was quite alarmed,
And put it with the other eggs to get it nice and warmed.
They kept a careful watch upon that egg while it was hatching
And it wasn't very long before they heard a happy scratching.
However, when the chick emerged, they were quite unsuspecting
That it would not exactly be what they had been expecting.
Now many folk would say to them "Adapt yourselves to change.
Accept things as they come to you no matter if they're strange."
But should they raise this foundling just as if it were their own,
They'd find their child would eat them up as soon as it was grown.

The Speech Lesson

"Baby must pronounce her proper name,"
Said Pop to Mama Hippopotamus.
"She should not babble such a lot-a-mus,
It's giving me a headache, we are both to blame.
We must rid her of her hippo-stutter-us,
She's old enough to know what's-what-erus.
I'm telling you, it puts us all to shame.
She must practice like our first-begot-a-mus
To say 'My name is Hippopotamus.'
Why, that's the proudest thing a child can claim."

The Truth about Pets

If you want the truth about pets,
To tell you will not take all day.
Your dog will come when you call him;
Your cat will just walk away.

Lightning Bug

I come to the dark fields, I dive from the sky.
Moon dancing, moon dancing, I flicker and fly.
With my wings for a sail, and a light for a tail,
And the night for a sea. Watch for me! Watch for me!

A Zoo Keeper

A zoo keeper studied hypnosis,
And decided to try lesson one.
He unlocked a couple of cages,
Thinking that he'd have some fun.
He did get the animals staring,
But he hadn't read lesson two.
A few of the beasts quickly taught him
That his education was through.

On Flying a Kettle

There never was
A wind so strong
You could get in a kettle
And fly it.
But my hat's off to you
Or anyone who
Decided to
Actually try it.

Ode to One Who Sleeps Late

Do not fault the lazy man
Who chooses to rise late.
He may achieve his destiny
By sleeping through his fate.

The Truth about Jack Horner

Remember Jack Horner
Who sat in a corner eating his pie?
And he put in his thumb
And he pulled out a plum
And said, "What a good boy am I?"
I know you'll be shocked when I tell you
That the story never was true.
For a hundred years all the books said so,
No wonder the legend grew.
What really happened was all hushed up
And lost to history
For fear it would scare the children
Since it ended so violently.
The real truth is, Jack's thumb got caught,
And the pie would not let go.
No matter how he pushed and pulled,
It stayed stuck in the dough.
Then suddenly, with no forewarner,
It was the *pie* that ate Jack Horner!

The Moogly Mugfords

Long ago there lived some folk
Known as Moogly Mugfords.
They were friends to the Gelphs and the Gurks.
But I know no more than this
For they left no lasting works.
Their heads were pointed so they say,
Their legs were bowed and bandy.
But they all dressed up
On Friday night
And my,
Didn't they
Look dandy!

Earth Speak

Two spies from Mars were sent to Earth
To study Earthmen's conversation.
They landed in a soccer field
During physical education.
Two third grade boys were on the lot,
In argument both fierce and hot.
And all the Martians ever got
Was: "Poop on you!"
"Vomit and Rot!"
"Booger! Booger! Booger!"
"Snot! Snot! Snot!"

My Joke

I told my friend my funniest joke,
He laughed so hard his glasses broke.
His eyes grew wide, he grinned with glee,
He chuckled, "Ha, Ha, Hee, Hee, Hee."
He howled so loud he lost his voice.
It looked so very queer
To see his mouth go up and down
Yet not a sound to hear.
I watched as tears rolled down his face,
Geez, he was barely breathing.
The way he made his elbows flap
Was half-way past believing.
With horror I just watched him
For I could not help at all.
He groaned and twitched, his face turned red,
He banged his head against the wall.
He beat his fists upon his desk,
His legs began to dance.
Unable to control himself,
The poor guy wet his pants.
Yellow sloop ran down his nose,
He snickered in his drool.
The teacher then called 9-1-1,
And they took him out of school.
The class was in a state of shock,
Nobody moved, nobody spoke.
And since that day I've been afraid
To ever tell another joke

I Lost My Head

This morning it was very weird,
When I woke up I had no head.
I could not see a single thing
Or hear a word my mother said.
I could not see my pants or shirt
So I had trouble dressing.
Lucky I could feel the buttons
Or it would have been distressing.
I could not eat my breakfast,
Not even toast or butter.
I could not blow my nose,
Not one sound could I utter.
Please believe me when I say
To lose your head is not too cool.
I had to hold my sister's hand
So I could find my way to school.
Previously it's been suggested
I am not a handsome dude.
Max said, flat out, I'm ugly,
But he's known for being crude.
Still, it was a big concern,
What would they call me now?
Without a head to call my own,
I had no eyes, no nose, no brow.
Turns out I shouldn't have worried
What all my friends would say.
They just asked what was I doing
That I looked so good today.

The Game

A cat once had a clever thought,
He'd pretend to be a painting.
He put his head through a canvas screen
And, still as stone, stood waiting.
Soon two mice strode idly by,
And trying to impress,
Each told the other how he thought
The painting was a mess.
"The artist has the head all wrong,"
Laughed one, "the ears are funny."
"Yes, I agree," the other said.
"They look more like a bunny."
"It's unrealistic," claimed the first.
"The eyes look very queer."
"Yes, to be sure," his friend agreed,
"The drawing is not clear.
There's something to the mouth, as well,
That doesn't look quite right."
With that,
The cat leaped
From the frame
And ate them
In one bite.
The lesson is:
One's ignorance
Will likely
Be displayed
When one does not
Exactly know
What game
Is being played.

40

Caroline's Quandary

You can ponder over everything,
Ask questions, and try to think through it.
But in the end, you still don't know,
Should you, or shouldn't you, do it.

Peter the Lighthouse Keeper

A lighthouse keeper I shall be,
A keeper of the light,
A beacon in the night.
A watcher on the rocks I'll be
For those who founder on the sea.
Go safely, little boat, and do not fear.
My friendly light will warn when you are near!
These rocks are dangerous to thy brave sail
Lost out there in the fog,
Blown out there by the gale.

Market Day

I took two geese to market
And got one dollar each.
Two quarters bought a baseball,
One penny bought a peach.
I also had enough to buy
A heavy sack of wheat.
I sold that to a grocer
For two dollars
On the street.
With my two dollars
Back in hand,
I bought a rubber ball.
I sold that for a dollar
As I bounced it on the wall.
I had two dollars once again,
And wondered what to buy.
I wandered all about the square
But nothing caught my eye
Until I spied my own two geese.
Why, just the thing thought I.
I paid the man just what he asked,
Two dollars wasn't much to pay,
Thinking as I walked back home,
This certainly was my lucky day.

I Heard a Sound

I heard a scary sound,
Whatever can that be?
Perhaps some hideous creature
Is sneaking up on me.
Whoa, there goes that sound again,
It was creepy, like a ghost.
Maybe it could be a snake,
I'm scared of them the most.
I don't like spiders either,
But they wouldn't make *that* sound.
It might could be a grizzly bear
That's crawling on the ground.
The sound was kind of like a scritch,
And then I heard a plinct.
I know it's not a dinosaur
Because they are extinct.
No matter what that monster is
I've got to be prepared
To look him right straight in the eye
And show him I'm not scared!

The Escape

"Don't look now" said brother rat,
"I think I can I smell a cat.
Come on let's go, let's leave, let's flee
Before he sinks his teeth in me.
If you don't care about *your* skin
Then think about the fix *I'm* in.
What will my wife and children do
If I end up as some cat chew?
Come on, be quick. Don't breathe. Don't squeal.
Or this could be our final meal!"

I'm So Mad

I'm mad, mad, mad.
I'm really, really mad.
I'm wild-man, mean-man
Mad, mad, mad.
I'm mad-machine mad,
Yell-and-scream mad,
Mad-extreme mad
Mad, mad, mad.

I'm spit-out-nails mad,
Chew-rats'-tails mad,
Mad-explode mad,
Overload mad!
Mad, mad, mad, mad,
Bad, bad, bad mad.
Oh, I am so mad
Mad, mad, mad!

Tanner

When Tanner goes for ice cream,
He always takes his time.
There are so many flavors:
Orange, and lemon-lime,
Chocolate fudge and chocolate chip,
Coconut, and cherry,
Brownie fudge, and peanut crunch,
Rainbow, boysenberry,
Chocolate cheesecake, apple crisp,
Mango, peach-a-roos.
There are so many flavors,
However will he choose?
Then, finally, the clerk looks down,
"What will it be, Young Fella?"
The time had come to make his choice.
What did he pick? Vanilla.

The King has Lost his Castle

The King has lost his castle,
The Queen has lost her crown.
It must have been a mighty wind
To topple such extreme reknown.

The Fate of Benjamin Foy

Consider the fate of Benjamin Foy,
A perfectly terrible, horrible boy!
"No" was the only word he knew
When his parents had a chore to do.
No matter what his teachers asked,
He said "No" to every task.
They couldn't give homework to the fellow.
"No! Won't do it!" he would bellow.
Even at his birthday feast
The boy behaved
   just like a beast.
They offered him cake
   and ice cream, too.
He opened his mouth
   to say "Please,
   Thank you."
But his habit was
   of deep ingrain.
Before he could think
   to stop his brain,
The wretched child,
   to his great woe,
Could only scream
   and holler
  "NO!"

The Vain Rooster

The folks in the barnyard were late waking up,
But they served the rooster hot soup in a cup
When he told them his throat had just been too sore
To crow when the sun rose, as always before.
The rooster apologized to them all
For being protective and vain of his call.
"Forgive me that I am so proud of my crow
But it's always been my best feature you know."

The Thing about Pigs Is

A pig can go shopping
In silk and in satin.
A pig can be well-versed
In English and Latin.
A pig with a racquet
Can win every game.
A pig can go far if he's
In the fast lane.
But the thing about pigs is,
A near one or far one-
The thing about pigs is,
That they always *are* one.

When the Bough Breaks

Rock-a-bye baby on the tree top
When the wind blows, the cradle will rock.
I understand the nursery rhyme,
The picture's clear, the words are fine.
But what kind of idiots, tell me please,
Would hang their babies up in trees?

The Coolest Guy

He has the highest grades in school,
All the guys think he's so cool.
All the girls think he's extreme.
He's captain of the soccer team,
And usually makes the winning score.
He volunteers to help the poor.
He looks just like a movie star,
He's in a band, he plays guitar.
He won the county spelling bee,
His father won the lottery.
He's known as a computer whiz
And always aces every quiz.
His birthday party's out of sight—
They shoot off fireworks at night.
He's brave, there's nothing
He won't try, and
He couldn't be a nicer guy.
He even lets his little sis berate him,
The guy is perfect.
I just hate him.

There Once Lived a Woman

There once lived a woman
Mean as fright
Who swept out her cats
On a snowy night.
She did not care
If they starved or froze,
And that's how mean
That woman was.

My Best Friend Moved to Boston

My best friend moved to Boston
And I'm too big to cry.
But school will never be the same,
It's like they moved the sky.
Now I know the meaning of bereft.
It means that you're the one they've left.

I Can't Remember

I can't remember, thought the rat,
The last time that I saw that cat.
Don't hear him purring, oh dear me,
That cat will be the death of me.
He might be underneath the sink,
I can't go in the kitchen.
He is awfully close I think,
My whiskers are all twitching.
That murderous beast would eat me up
Until nothing's left at all
Except a wee bit of my tail
Or a piece of tooth or claw.
Oh, I must hurry to my nest,
The hair upon my back just rizz.
I have to leave this room right now.
I heard that cat and THERE HE IS!

The Monster Max Drew

Max once drew a monster
With two great staring eyes,
And a grizzled mouth with pointed teeth
Of quite enormous size.
Max worked so hard on the hideous grin
He ran quite out of breath.
Then he looked down at what he'd drawn,
And scared himself to death.

Parade!

Nobody now remembers the cause of the commotion,
But down the street the townsmen came as if they had a notion
To scare us all out of our wits with noise and rife confusion!
Farmer Fred stood on his head, and then in strange collusion,
Banker Thole a wagon stole.
Quite merrily he sped,
Though with the other
   carryings on,
None heard
   a word he said.
Merchant Greer
   brought up the rear
While pulling
   Dobbin's tail.
The dogs all barked,
The geese all quacked.
The Captain called for ale.
Why Brother Howe
   would ride the cow
I never did hear mention.
Some people will
   do anything
Just to attract
   attention.

In a Bull's Eye

Bob told her to wait on the sidelines
For his archery class to be done.
But the sidelines were whizzing with arrows
That kept Jane full-time on the run.
She noticed at last there was one place
Where an arrow just never came near,
So she sat down in front of the target
Where she knew she had nothing to fear.

Mrs. Dog Goes Shopping

There was no bread for breakfast,
No crumb did meet her eye.
So Mrs. Dog went shopping,
And what then did she buy?
Why some powder and some poultice,
Some nice blueberry pie.
Some ribbon and some thread,
And a needle for to sew it.
A smallish wooden sled
With steel runners
Down below it.
A cradle and a ladle,
A pot of beefy stew.
Some strong and sweet
Blackberry wine,
A cookie box or two.
But when she got home
She'd forgotten the bread.
No matter, she thought,
I will bake some instead.

Seven Times Nine

I couldn't remember
Seven times nine,
So I wrote it on my knee.
And though it washed off long ago,
I still remember it's 63.

Halloween's Coming

October is here and Halloween's soon,
And many a witch will ride out on her broom,
Flying over the mountains and over the dales
With her grisly groans and her hideous wails.

The Witches

What shall I put
In my witches' brew?
A long slimy eel,
And a dead rat, or two!
Perhaps an old toad,
And a yellow snake belly,
Sweetened perhaps
With some mulberry jelly.
A gizzard, two lizards,
A mushroom, some glue,
Two pairs of old socks,
And one smelly shoe.
I'll throw in some mud,
Then I'll boil it and baste it,
And when I'm all through
You can come here and taste it.

The Old Witch and Mr. Wizard

The Old Witch invited her friend Mr. Wizard
To join her for lunch in spite of the blizzard.
They ordered the dragon scales and raw lizard,
And happily munched on the bones, blood, and gizzard.
All around them were roaring the wind, snow and hail,
And the café was starting to pitch in the gale.
"We must hurry," the witch said, "the lights may soon fail.
Eat the eyes, my good friend, and I'll finish the tail."

Turtle Ride

To ride a turtle is complex, they pull into their shell.
Try putting cabbage on a stick, some think that works quite well.
But even when you're going good, those legs could duck in fast
And leave you stranded, rolling off, and sitting on the grass.
And one thing more that's even worse, they will not go into reverse.

I'm blowing bigger bubbles every day,
I make them with this magic pipe I found.
I'll soon make one that's big enough to ride,
Then I'll float up and have a look around.

The Twins are Eating Ice Cream

The twins are eating their ice cream sundae,
For being so good they got a fun day.
But when they get to that last bite,
Those two spoons are going to fight!

When the Crocodiles Come

Better run
when the
crocodiles
come.

Better hide
when the
crocodiles
glide.

Better dash
when the
crocodiles
splash.

Better
beat
your feet
when the
crocodiles
eat.

The Sand-Hill Crane

When the sand-hill crane
Comes walking
Along the river beach,
The frogs and fish
All scurry
To get out of
His reach.
They really rush
To beat him
'Cause if they don't,
He'll eat 'em.

Flamingoes

Why do those flamingoes
Basking in the sun,
Who have two perfectly good legs,
Only stand on one!?

My Dog is Terribly Dignified

My dog is terribly dignified, he has no ticks or fleas.
He always kindly tips his hat to everyone he sees.
My dog is terribly dignified, he has no fleas or ticks,
And would not think of traveling without his walking sticks.

A Boater Named Dale

There once was a boater named Dale
Who used window shades for a sail.
Were the wind high or low,
He'd roll up, or let go;
And thus never ditched in a gale

During the Last Tornado

During the last tornado
The winds rose up so high
That we were kept quite busy
With friends who kept dropping by.

Caught by a Book

Mom dropped me off at the bookstore
To check out the new reading nook.
One of the titles was *Don't Open Me*,
So, of course, I snuck me a look.
Now I know what they mean when they say
"I got all caught up in a book."

It Can't be Done

The frog was quite insistent,
So the argument he won:
Bicycles made of daisies
Was a thing that couldn't be done.
But the work at hand was nicely planned;
Darned if that bug didn't stick it.
Next thing frog knew he was bumped into
By a petal-riding cricket.

The New Sail

His rigging was so perfect
He was moving right along.
But as the little boater sailed,
Back home things had gone wrong.
After looking in her closet,
His mother, in great stress,
Was lamenting to the household,
"Who's stolen my best dress!"

Old Man in a Boat

There was an old man in a boat
Who found himself failing to float.
When the water arose almost to his nose
He called out for help with a shout.
When nobody came, he still was quite game,
And punched in some holes so the water ran out.

Erma's Mistake

Her mother warned her that pigs don't fly.
When she tried, it turned bad for Erma.
She was lassoed and hooked,
Her bacon was cooked.
She shouldn't have left terra firma.

A Boy from Deloot

There once was a boy from Deloot
Who rode on a basket of fruit.
This very strange horse
Bucked him off in due course,
And he ended up on his patoot.

The Flying Peregrine

There once was a strange boy called Peregrine
Who wanted to fly in the air again.
He first tried a kite,
A balloon wasn't right,
But a pirate's chest soon got him there again.

There Once was a Soldier

There once was a soldier named Zane
Who rode with the army in Spain.
The unfortunate fella
So loved his umbrella
He wouldn't come in out of the rain.

Three Men from Ah-so-shun

There once were three men from Ah-so-shun
Who wanted to study the ocean.
They rode off on a fish,
Ended up in a ditch.
But we credit them for their devotion.

Three Men from U-kind-it

Three men bought a house in U-kind-it.
A tornado then redesigned it.
Though at first quite perturbed
That their porch was disturbed,
They soon became higher minded.

Rickity Tickity Tight

Rickity tickity tight,
Kyle tied his cat to a kite.
It dragged him high
Into the sky,
And he hasn't been seen
Since Saturday night.

No Way of Knowing

There is no way of knowing
If what you're going to do
Is going to turn out well,
Or roast you in some stew.
But always risk adventure
No matter how you end up.
Cause risk makes all the difference,
And you can always mend up.

The Secret of Life

Chances come and chances go.
So, as you're going through it,
The thing about Life to remember is,
You personally have to do it.

Please Forgive Me

It takes one second, and two little words.
It's the most important thing we never say.
Because it's harder to say "I'm sorry"
Than "Good luck," or "Have a nice day."

Learning to Fly

"Jump! Jump!" said Mama bird,
"Spread your wings and fly."
But baby bird clung to the branch
And fear was in his eye.
"Come on, come on," his mother urged
"Enough of this boo-hoo-it.
Every bird is born to fly,
Why there is nothing to it.
One little hop is all you need
To fly the sky with all the rest."
"If you don't mind," said baby bird
"I think I'd rather fly the nest."

The Contest

Don't even try
To stare me down.
My eyes are wide
In frozen frown.
I will not smile,
I will not think,
I will not be
The first to blink.

All the Answers

My teacher asked me if I'd like
To always know the answer
To every question in the world.
I told him "Not a chance, Sir.
I don't know much geography
But I'm not such a dunce.
A hundred ninety four countries
Might call me all at once.
If every head of state called me
Each day, wouldn't that be fine?
Each morning I'd be late to school,
I'd never be on time.
Just our country by itself
I know has fifty states.
Times two senators for each
Would raise my cell phone rates.
Representatives in Congress
Are four hundred thirty five.
They'd all be calling me as well,
You know how they connive.
Let us leave things as they are,
My brain is now a work of art.
Leave wisdom to the wise, and I'll stay
Not too dumb, and not too smart.

The Wimpy Child

NO FAIR!
They made me late. They made me cry.
They stuck their finger in my eye.
They called me names, won't let me play.
It was my turn, they said, "No way."
Take him out to the woods
And toss him to the wild.
There's nothing worse than a wimpy child.

Emily Demily Dithery Daw

Emily Demily Dithery Daw,
Was the laziest child I ever saw.
She stayed in bed 'til half past noon,
She washed her cup but not her spoon.
She made her breakfast but not her bed,
Ate her butter but not her bread.
She fed the dog but not the cat,
Put on her coat but not her hat.
She's still in the house at half past four
'Cause she opened the windows
But not the door.

Beware the Elephant

Look out when the elephant
Stumps and stomps!
You better beware when he
Bumps and bomps.
You better be quick when he
Rumps and romps.
When he makes a terrible ruckus,
You better watch your tuckus!

How Could I?

How could I
Have said that?
I looked like
Such a chump.
I could have kept
My big mouth shut,
But in I had to jump!
I had to give
My two cents worth,
I had to act so smart.
When everybody
Laughed at me,
It tore me right apart.
From now on
I will think ahead,
And then
I'll count to ten
Before I ever, ever say
Such a stupid thing again.

Rain

Last night it rained.
The windows got wet,
The doors got wet.
The churches got wet,
The stores got wet.
The trees got wet,
The roads got wet.
The bees got wet,
The toads got wet.
The cats got wet,
The dogs got wet.
The skunks got wet,
The hogs got wet.
But drip drop dret,
I'm not wet yet

Too Big for his Britches

John Parker Pratt put on his daddy's hat,
Put on his daddy's jacket, just like that.
He then put on his daddy's boots, and felt so very tall
He tried to boss his sister, who liked it not at all.
His mother had to ground him from his self-exalted station,
A lesson to the rest of us to know our limitation.

Solmar Was a Skinny Kid

When Solmar was a skinny kid,
It gave me great delight
To call him names and punch him out
Since I won every fight.
But when he grew to six foot three,
I suddenly became polite.

A Boy Called Wolf

Wolf has got a will of iron,
Wolf has got a mind of steel.
He always knows the story
And he cuts the deal.
If Wolf don't want his breakfast,
He just won't eat,
Though you stick him with needles
Or hang him by his feet.
If Wolf don't want to tell you
Something that he knows,
You can wait around forever
Just cooling your toes.

My Cousin Summer

She put a basket on her head,
And said it was her hat.
She used a broom for baseball,
And hit a homer with her bat.
She didn't eat her Easter egg,
It turned into a hen.
She scolded her dog only once,
It never barked again.
Once she caught a rabbit,
And said it was her cat–
But that's how Summer is.
She is just *like* that!

Paula

Paula has the bluest eyes,
She has the prettiest hair.
She's kind to everyone she meets,
She's honest, loyal, and fair.
She's practically a perfect child,
Cheerful, sweet, and glad.
But take a little hint from me,
Don't ever make her mad.

Ten Years Old

That Dratted Fly

I tried to catch that dratted fly,
And slammed him in my book.
No bloody carcass did I spy
When I peeked in to look.
But NO! I heard his nasty buzz,
And I looked up
And there he was.

I waited till he lighted,
And thwacked him with a POW!
I was quite delighted
That I had got him now.
But NO! I heard his nasty buzz,
And I looked down
And there he was.

Drat, he flew away again
So I sat down to dinner.
My timing was just perfect,
Thus I turned out the winner.
HO HO!! I heard his nasty buzz
Fly in my mouth,
And there he was.

CRUNCH!

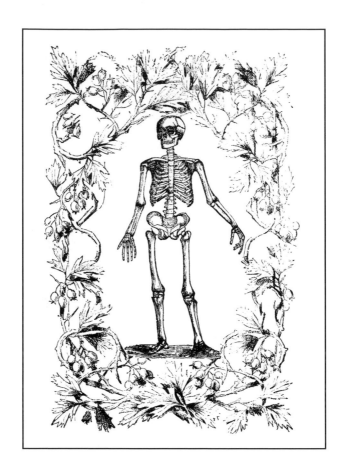

When it Comes to Beer and Whisky

When it comes to beer and whiskey,
"No" is safe and "Yes" is risky.
There's many a fellow has met his due
By bending his elbow to quaff his brew.

Litterture

Only a cur writes doggerel.
Only hungry people write pooretry.
Only childish people write plays,
And only miners do oretry.

My Cousins are Coming

My cousins are coming, Cutter and Tanner,
Roll out the carpet and unfurl the banner.
My cousins are coming, Tanner and Cutter,
Get out the jam and peanut butter.
My cousins are coming! My cousins are coming!
We can play drums, and bam, bam, bam
With Cutter, Cut, Cut and Tanner, Tan, Tan.
My cousins are coming! My cousins are coming!
We can play soldier and hut, hut, hut
With Tanner, Tan, Tan and Cutter, Cut, Cut.

The Groaning

You can always tell a Groaning
By the way he's always moaning,
Approach his cave if you dare.
He's so big you know,
That each little toe
Has to have its own private chair.
His eyes are round, he has a snout,
He growls just like a bear.
Oh, I do wish you could see one,
But they are extremely rare.

The New Dog

One day we got a new dog, Rascal was his name.
He seemed a little lonesome for his old home,
But otherwise quite mannerly and tame.
Dad started in to growling with his early morning gruff,
"That DOG is gonna stay OUTSIDE!"
Wolf, thinking Dad was being kind of tough,
Practically sat right down and cried.
Mom said, "It will work out, but didn't want to boss him
When Dad was so insistent. And Wolf was scared to cross him.
So Mom was quiet, Dad looked mad.
The dog outside looked small and sad.
"Please, Dad, can he sleep in my room just tonight?"
"AB~SO~LUTE~LY~NO~aw~well~all~right."

Hunting with John McGrew

When you go hunting with John McGrew,
You do whatever he tells you to.
When the lions come,
Grab a gun. Quick-ly.
And look them in the eye,
And you better not cry.
That's the worst thing you can do.

Run for Your Life

Run for your life!
Oh me! Oh my!
The sun has fallen from the sky.
Run for your life!
They'll be no noon.
Thank goodness we
Still have the moon.

Mavrik's Stair

"Of course," Mavrik said, "I can get it myself.
I see the darn thing right there on the shelf."
But the shelf was too high
So he got a chair.
Still too high
So he got a bear.
Still too high
So he got a mare.
Still too high
So he got a pear
And made a stair
To get up there.

Cutter Concentration

I can still see Cutter
On that day.
Deep in the field,
He watched the play.
The ball was hit,
The batter ran;
So does Cutter,
Fast as he can.
I thought he would miss,
But he leaps fot it.
He catches that ball
In the palm of his mitt
While stretched flat out
Like a Frisbee in flight
Sailing on air.
It was such a great sight!
Then he lands with a thud
In the dirt and the sand
But he never lets go
Of that ball in his hand.

Harmony Rose

Harmony Rose sparkles rings on her toes.
Necklaces dangle wherever she goes.
She dances with fire, and with fireflies,
And speaks to the moon with serious eyes,
Like some fairy princess, here in disguise.

Blueray Belury

What can I say about Blueray Belury?
He's a cool guy, he's not in a hurry.
He's way laid back, nothing disturbs him.
Can't get on his nerves, nothing perturbs him.
It's not that we haven't tried to upset him.
Just nothing we've found seems ever to fret him.

Doodle Bugs

Do doodle bugs sing?
Do doodle-bugs dance?
Do doodle-bugs play
With spiders, or ants?
Do doodle-bugs live
In England, or France?
Are they bugs that live in water
Or bugs that live in plants?
Are they very, very scared bugs
Or would they take a chance?
Are they brave "Yes, yes, I can" bugs
Or are they "No, I can'ts?"

Her Mother Said

"Don't take your umbrella out today,"
Her mother warned, "It's windy."
But the child just never listens,
So there goes Cousin Cindy.

Watch Out!   By Peregrine Curtiss   Age 11

Summertime and the water is warm.
Invite some friends to the beach.
But when evening strikes and you're surfing,
Make sure you stay out of reach.

At Hole-in-the-Wall, sharks are vicious.
Your flesh to them is delicious.
They'll eat anything from a tire to you,
And say "Thanks for the arm, don't mind if I do."

But luckily, I am quick on my board,
And I'm not scared of sharks, oh please!
My fins are sharper than any sword
And they'll slice through the sharks like cheese

Untrustworthy

I don't have the nerve to tell you the truth,
I wish I were more than I am.
But, cross my heart, I promise to tell you
The littlest lie that I can.

The Mystery of Life

Life is a journey of events,
But only hindsight can connect 'em
Into meaningful conclusion
Of causes and effectum.

Proud as a Peacock

Too much bragging and boasting
Puts your social neck in a noose.
Being proud as a peacock
Can pretty much cook your own goose.

Humility

If you see a beggar on the street,
With nowhere to go and nothing to eat,
You might even think to pass him by
As if you do not see him.
But offer up a little prayer
That you're lucky not to be him.
For maybe there's a universe
That's opposite to this one,
And you may be the beggar there
And not the other which one.

Old John and his Wife

Old John and his wife talk of this and of that.
"Have you noticed the weather?"
"Mind the dog."
"Watch the cat."
"Do your chilblains feel better?"
"Is your knitting near done?"
"I must get a new cane."
"My old stocking's run."
And there's never a quarrel, and never a spat
When Old John and his wife talk of this and of that.

The Little Gossips

I said, "But we're just talking."
And Mom said, "No. That's gossip!"
The other day when my friend was here
My Mom told us to "Stop it!"
She says we shouldn't be talking mean
About our friends at school.
She says we are forgetting
About the golden rule.
But it's so hard remembering
When I'm in a cozy chat.
Maybe an elephant never forgets,
But I'm more like a cat.
So Mom gave me this little test
To use when I'm in doubt.
How would I feel
If I were that little girl
I was talking about?

On Dining with a Peccary

There's a problem with the peccary
As he dines on a lost calf or dog.
His unpardonable taste and deplorable haste
Don't encourage polite dialogue.

Watching a Hummingbird

To keep your eye on a hummingbird
You must concentrate like you mean it.
For, suspended in flight,
He can flit from your sight
And you wonder if you've even seen it.

The World is Full of Sky

The world is full of sky and trees.
The clouds blow softly in the breeze.
The little birds, since break of day,
Have called the morning out to play.

When Knights in Armor

When knights in armor battle,
They crash and clank and clattle.
To yells and shouts that each employs,
Their horses raise more dust and noise.
With all the turmoil, thrash and din,
You wonder how they know they win.

So Many Shoes

There was a man who had
So many boots and shoes
That he never could get dressed
For not knowing which to choose.

The Starfish

Mavrik saw starfish everywhere, they were dying on the shore.
He'd toss one back into the surf, then see a dozen more.
"You can't save all these starfish, Boy,"
A man said with a sigh.
"Must be thousands of them here,
It makes no sense to try."
The little hero saw right through such bleak analysis.
"But I can save this one," he said,
"And this, and this, and this."

The Brave Cat

"I'm not afraid of you," hissed the brave cat.
And the dog just sat.
"My teeth are razor sharp," hissed the brave cat.
And the dog just sat.
"I can scratch your eyes out," hissed the brave cat.
And the dog just sat.
But then the sleeping dog woke up
And that was that.
The brave cat disappeared
In just three seconds flat.

Anger Management

No one wants to hear you scream,
And watch your anger go extreme!
Sanity is not a gift from Heaven.
If ten is not enough, count to eleven!

Shelli, the Optimist

The river is flooding through town
But nothing gets our Shelli down.
No matter what goes bad or wrong,
She'll say she's "Sailing right along!"

Molly's Perfect Day

Molly had a perfect day, it happened for no reason.
It wasn't any holiday or any special season.
There was a promise of excitement
As she felt soft breezes blow.
The world was like a present tied with a sunshine bow.
Oh, *anything* was possible, *anywhere* she'd go.

Making Music

Don't fret if you don't have a drum,
No fiddle, short or stout.
If you have music in your soul,
It will find its own way out.

Contentment

Some butter and bread
And my nice old cat,
Why would anybody
Want more than that?

Sadness is beautiful because
People are so incredibly important.

His Own

Each has his own,
As thee hath thine.
I love my goose
Because she's mine.

A Bird Lives Lightly on the Earth

A bird lives lightly on the Earth
In simple nests of twigs or hay.
He leaves behind no monuments of berth,
Just elegant memories of his stay.

The Robin and the Bluebell

"Come with me," the Robin said, "and fly around a bit."
"Sorry," said the Bluebell, "flowers were born to sit."
"Oh dear," began the little bird, "I want to fly around,
And cross the river, see the sights, not stay here on the ground."
"That's quite okay," the Bluebell said, "You go and don't mind me.
Look around, and then come back and tell me what you see.
Knowing you, you'll bob and weave, flying fast and furious.
You'll come back and tell me all. Then, is it not curious?
You'll put your head beneath your wing and sleep, too tired to care,
While my imagination will then fly me everywhere!"

Music is not weighed for worth.
The smallest of songs is welcome on Earth.

Your looking glass reflects the mirror of your mind.
You never will be beautiful if you cannot be kind.

This is a Lesson

This is a lesson for fish and you:
As a fish thinketh so shall he do.
This is a lesson for fish and thee:
As a fish doeth, so shall he be.

The Pitiful Truth

Somtimes things will happen
In a way you never planned.
Do not cling to lies and excuses,
(Though you won't be looking grand.)
This is the time for courage!
And there's no more noble stand
Than to face your accusers with nothing
But your pitiful truth in your hand.

Sweet Tooth

I eat more sweet things than I should.
I know they are not good for me,
The thing is that they taste so good!
Perhaps I'm being tested and found wanting
But the thought of eating spinach is, well, daunting!

The River

The river so joyfully moves along,
It murmurs deep where the current is strong.
It lightly sings over pebble and stone
The song of the wilderness going home.

When I Forget

When I forget there's a world out there,
And I'm feeling alone and glum,
It sends me soft and gentle winds,
And then all these little stars come.

I think I have a hundred faces,
I find them in the strangest places.

Evening Tea

When evening tea is by the fire,
And the cat has ceased to roam,
Take off your coat, put up the day.
It's time to rest, you're home!

The Wind

Have you ever thought
How the wind is alone,
And wanders forever,
And never goes home?

Perfect Day

Have you ever had such a perfect day
You wanted to save it and put it away,
Lock it up in a box like a precious gem,
So you could have it forever, again?

The Majesty of An Elephant

There is majesty in an elephant
That silently stands in place,
Like some ever-evolving consciousness
Has come to a state of grace.

The World

The world so wraps around us
That all creatures may abide.
I am safe and warm within,
And the wolf is safe outside.

Aubrey's Decision

They say your cage is now too small.
I don't think you need one at all.
There is no cage as big as being free.
Fly away little bird, remember me.

Trouble

Trouble is not like molasses,
Moving along by the minute.
Trouble is much more like quicksand~
All of a sudden you're in it!

The Creative Spirit

If you're not set on approbation,
You will avoid the agitation
Of unrealistic expectation
That is the death of innovation.

Pardon me, please, I'd like to say
That same thing another way:

If you can take the risk
Of looking like a jerk
You'll be able to
Make anything work!

Positive Action

I will not cry another minute.
I'll look at the day and see what's in it.
I'll brush my teeth, and make my bed.
If I'm still not happy, I'll stand on my head.

In for a Penny

Once you've made up your mind
And taken your ground,
If you're in for a penny,
You're in for a pound.
There's no turning back
When you've taken your shot.
If you're in for a little,
You're in for the lot.

Can I Do It?

"Can I do it? Can I do it?
If I really want to do it?
If I'm not sure I can do it
'Cause I'm scared?" said Ben.

You can do it, you can do it,
If you think that you can do it.
You can do it! You can do it,
If you only think you can.

"Wow! I did it cause I did it!
I did it cause I did it!
If I ever want to do it,
I'll just do it again."

Your Dream

It's good to have a dream.
And I also think it is true,
That if you believe in your dream,
Then your dream will believe in you.

A Rat in Every Barnyard

There's a rat in every barnyard,
They never do anyone good.
Why they exist at all
Goodness knows!
Maybe just to keep us
On our toes.

When I Can't Decide

When I can't decide if it's this or that,
I talk it over with my cat.
When I can't decide if it's now or then,
I talk it over with my hen.
The only trouble I ever see
Is when the two do not agree.

The Flowers are There

Here's a bit of wisdom
Straight from the flower pot:
The flowers are always there,
Whether your window is open or not.

A doctor shouldn't study the things on his shelf
Without ever turning the glass on himself

If You Know How to Dance

From New York to Boston,
From England to France,
You don't need to be humble
If you know how to dance.

The Truth

There's no greater truth,
It's clear as a bell.
If you do something wrong,
Somebody will tell!

Frog Philosophy

His skin so green and scaly,
His voice so cracked and dry,
I could not help but pity him,
To which Frog did reply:
"My friend, as you like being you,
I'm glad that I am I."

Don't Live a Life of Dog Eat Dog

Don't live a life of dog eat dog.
What kind of life is that?
While you're busy whomping some smaller guy,
Like a cat will bully a rat,
You might not notice some bigger dog
Getting ready to knock you flat.

Tanner's Mouse Story

Once upon a time there lived a little mouse
Who was born into an ordinary house.
His family led a boring and an uneventful life.
There was a regular, ordinary kind of husband,
And a regular, ordinary kind of wife.
There were sisters, and there also were some brothers.
But they were kind of ordinary too.
But not that little mouse, no, he was different.
But in that boring house, what could he do?
However, he held onto dreams of glory,
And vowed to live in manner much more brisk.
His scheme and plan was that he soon would run off
To a life of great excitement and high risk.

Ashley's Answer

One day I figured out
Why the world
Is full of woe:
A plethora of stop,
A paucity of go.
A plethora of strings,
A paucity of ties.
A plethora of smarts,
A paucity of wise.
A plethora of groan,
A paucity of greet.
A plethora of mess,
A paucity of neat.
A plethora of books,
A paucity of time.
A plethora of wars,
A paucity of rhyme.
A plethora of won't,
A paucity of willing.
A plethora of need,
A paucity of filling.

What could we say
When silly Auntie Sly
Went to buy geese
For her gooseberry pie?

Teodora's New Day

There's a whole new day outside:
I hear the new-day birds,
I see the new-day sky,
And the breeze is a new-day breeze.
And me, I'm a new-day I.

The Selfish Day

The moon fails as she throws her meager light
Around the shoulders
Of the spare and shivering Night.
How cold they go into the dawn,
While just below, the sun comes on.
Then Day plumps down as cozy as you please,
And sits in sunbeams warm as melted cheese.

What Word?

When I want to write you a note,
I never know where to start.
I never know what to say,
What word can tell you my heart?

How Ford Got His Name

Mom got his name from the telephone book,
Just opened it up and took the first look.
"What do you think of Ford," she said.
"I like it," Dad smiled, looking over the bed
At his newborn son. So "Ford" it would be,
And they never looked back.
And neither did he.

There Came Down the Road a Beggar

There came down the road a beggar,
Wailing and moaning his lot.
"No one's poorer than me," he said,
"Not a thing of worth have I got.
I've holes in my socks, and holes in my shoes,
My coat's too torn, and my hat's too bruised."
He threw down his hat with great disdain,
In the road he let it lay.
He kicked off his shoes, and tossed them aside;
In the dust they settled side by side.
He flung his coat both high and wide,
And the wind blew it quite away.
And what do you think did happen then?
Why the world barely turned around,
When right behind him another man,
As fast as he threw them down,
Was picking up the beggar's clothes,
Rejoicing at what he'd found.

Oh, Nothing!

Oh, Nothing's been bothering me lately.
I wish I knew what to do.
Oh, Nothing's been bothering me lately.
First it was just Oh, Nothing One,
But now it's Oh, Nothing Too.

Ode to the Futalognkosaurus

It's the biggest dinosaur they ever found,
All the papers were quick to announce it.
But the name that they gave it was so very hard
I never knew how to pronounce it.
So my teacher suggested I make up a song
For the FOO-ta-long-koh-SOHR-us
And since I wanted to learn it fast
I repeated the name in the chorus:

Eighty million years ago this creature lived before us.
He stands more than four stories high,
He's one humungus-saurus.
He's huge, more than one hundred feet,
Head to posteri-or-us
He has at least three hundred teeth,
But probably wouldn't gore us.
Even if he saw us, chances are he would ignore us.
He's mainly interested in plants because he's herbivorous.
This is the song, this is the song
Of the FOO-ta-long-koh-SOHR-us.
The FOO-ta-long, the FOO-ta-long,
The FOO-ta-long-koh-SOHR-us.

The Reader

I used to read my book near a hill,
On a rock warmed by the sun.
Oh, the schemes I schemed, and the dreams I dreamed,
Yes, I was the fancy one!
I was the fairy princess who always heard the words
That the winds blew, and the trees knew,
Oh, even the little birds.
I still can feel the magic when I read some favorite part,
Where the rhymes ring, and the words sing,
Oh, even the very heart!

An Explanation

The fact that vines
Grow out of seeds
Is hardly revelation.
But for why
There were seeds
In the first place
There is no explanation!

Go In Peace

The saddest thing that people say
When they reach that final door:
"I could have been a better person,
I could have done more."
But don't despair though you failed today,
Life starts anew tomorrow.
For each, whatever light we see
Is the light that we must follow.
Go in peace, there's just one test.
Rest easy, you have done your best.

The Columbia Space Shuttle

You took our nation to the stars,
How clear you shown against the sky.
A brighter trail has not been blazed,
That comet of your last goodbye.
We, who will never shine so bright,
Salute you braver eagles
On your heavenward flight.
As no star upon Old Glory ever dies,
Will you now fly forever
Wherever freedom flies.

The American Pioneer

Two hundred years ago you walked this land.
You walked alone, a stranger.
You held a small child by the hand.
No one caught you when you fell,
Or wept to see you fail.
You broke the soil, and lifted up the grain,
And left a trail to follow.
You shouldered a forest to build a cabin,
Log by log by log.
You had it done by winter
So you made it through the cold.
When you lost your corn to Summer,
And you lost your child to Fall,
With no place to go for turning back
You stood, and took it tall.
Then another came, and then another,
Strong, like you, then more,
To build a thousand cities
Where no city stood before.
You ached, and farmed the valley.
You strained, and mined the hill.
When hope died in your bosom,
It hardened into will.
You hammered a true nail.
You drew a straight plan.
You flew with the eagle
And you bowed to no man.

The Tao of History

How can we honor the Pioneers,
Knowing that they stole the lands
By killing off the Indian nations,
Scattering their remnant bands?
Yes, it is a quandary
But physics gives the clue.
There is no continuity,
Things only *seem* to be in two.
Each man is equally good and bad.
That's true of every nation.
That it is true for Pioneers
Should end our consternation.
Until you search to greater depth
These things are two: a foe, a friend.
Until you seek a higher ground
These things are two: the means, the end.
To reflect on Pioneers and Indians, and justice
Can cause the very mind to come undone,
Until you look beneath what can be seen,
And contemplate the Unseen,
Where Pioneers and Indians
And all of us
Are One.

The Indian and the White Man

The Indian shamans long foretold
Our coming to their shore,
To change the kind of life
That they had always known before.
Knowing this, the Indians fought us,
Knowing this, they bowed to peace.
Knowing this, they watched us burgeon,
As their own numbers decreased.
They deeply felt the sorrow
Of the dying of their race,
As the white man pushed them farther
To an ever distant place.
But they also knew their spirits
Never could be banned,
And would freely walk among us,
Who would settle on their land.
Though they don't care so much
For all our noisy, crowded places,
We can sometimes sense their presence
In the silent, open spaces.
"Be careful that you don't destroy
 All of our trees and plain.
For, if you do, than neither one of us
Can long remain."

Crossing the Delaware

In Seventeen Hundred and Seventy Six,
The first winter of our nation's birth,
George Washington's small Continental forces
Faced the greatest army on the earth.
His early count of twenty thousand men
Was down to but a fraction of that number.
The British claimed the war "already won."
Washington's own generals urged surrender.
"No! No!" the tireless leader cried, "We march!
We march though we must march both day and night.
It's freedom, men, it's freedom bids us fight."

The British had our forces on the run.
From every single stand did we retreat.
Hundreds killed and thousands more deserted,
Still, Washington would not admit defeat.
His ragged soldiers had just summer clothes,
Not even boots on many barefoot men
Who left their bloody footprints in the snow,
Who fell, rose up, only to fall again.
George Washington urged on his weary troops,
"We are the last defense, or freedom dies.
It's freedom, lads, it's freedom bids us rise."

On borrowed boats they crossed the Delaware.
His Continental troops could now revamp;
Our army on the other side of Trenton,
Where stood the stronghold of the Hessian camp.
But Hessians had the food and guns we needed.
The river was George Washington's advice.
In weeks, or days, he knew the British forces
With twenty thousand men would cross that ice.
His plan was that before the freeze would come,
He would suprise the Hessians, and recoup his loss.
"It's freedom, men, that bids us now re-cross."

How did they prevail--these farmers, boys, and fishermen
Against the Hessians' military might?
Some had only swords and bayonets to use,
And cannon fire and musket balls to fight.
And they were mostly young: fifteen, sixteen.
How could they do what generals could not do?
"We have no choice," their staunch commander urged,
"We are the last, we weary, hungry few."
On Christmas night they crossed the Delaware
Braved to their general's hail and battle's din.
"It's freedom, lads, it's freedom bids us win."

Another Note from the Author

Many of the poems in this part of the book, *The Brave Little Triplets*, came from small moments in the lives of my children when they were very young. For instance, the phrase "and the littlest one is last"on page 217 comes from this flash of memory. After dinner on a hot summer day, my first three children, Deane, Ford, and Demming are in the kitchen when Dad heads for the basement where we kept a large freezer, "Who's ready for their ice cream cone?"

Deane, the oldest boy yells out authoritatively, "First," and takes off on a run behind his father. Ford calls out competitively, "Second," and runs right behind his brother. Their baby sister, not quite three, and not to be left out of all the excitement, runs behind her big brothers lisping happily at the top of her little voice, "Yast!"

The Brave Little Triplets

The Brave Little Triplets

"We know a secret we won't tell,"
Said Reagan, McKay, and Kelsey Belle.
"Dragons are hiding under our bed
Though nobody *saw* them, and nobody *said.*

"But they're awful big, and frightful mean.
They're the terriblest monsters ever seen.
Each of their feet has twenty toes
That scritch and scratch wherever they goes.

"We hear them sneaking up the stairs
When we read our books and say our prayers.
We hear them roar, and breathe out fire.
Our hearts turn cold, our plight is dire.

"Who will save us from these beasts?
Will no one come when a monster shrieks?
Does no one hear, does no one see them?
Oh tell us, please, how we may flee them."

Then Kelsey says, "What do you think?
If we scared *them*, would they pounce or blink?
If we were very, very brave,
Maybe our own selves we could save."

"Okay," said Reagan, "Let's count to three,
Don't say a word and follow me."
So Reagan, McKay and Kelsey Bell
Marched straight to the room where the dragons dwell.

They tiptoed close, peeked through the door.
They saw no feet, they heard no roar.
Just to be sure, they all got ready;
McKay with blanket, Reagan with teddy.
Then they snuck in the room, and crept to the bed,
And looked underneath, and here's what they said:

"BOO!!"

Triplets

We've got babies by the triplets
That's how we're keeping score.
I'll bet you've never seen so many babies before!
They're coming in the window,
And they're knocking on the door.
I'll bet you've never seen so many babies before!
They're crawling up the stairway,
And they're rolling on the floor.
I'll bet you've never seen so many babies before!
Oh, we've got so many babies
But there's always room for more.
I'll bet you've never seen so many babies before!

When the Sun is Up

When the sun is up
The baby is up.
The sun and the baby are up, up, up.
When the sun is down
The baby is down.
The sun and the baby are down, down. down.

A Baby Can't

There are so many things
A baby can't do.
It can't button buttons,
It can't tie its shoe.
It can't say "Thank you,"
And it can't say "Please."
If you're older, like me,
You can do all of these.

If it Coos like a Baby

If it coos like a baby,
And crawls like a baby,
And wiggles, and squiggles,
And bawls like a baby;
If it laughs like a baby,
And squeaks like a baby,
And tumbles, and dribbles,
And leaks like a baby;
Well, maybe, maybe, maybe
It's a baby, baby, baby!

I'm Happy

I'm happy for my knees,
And I'm happy for my toes.
I'm happy for my eyes and ears.
Got two, of each, of those.
I'm happy for my shoes,
And I'm happy for my clothes.
I'm happy for the sun,
And I'm happy when it snows.
I'm happy for the bees,
And I'm happy for the rose.
And I'm happy when
You kiss me
On the top of my nose.

Ten Little Fingers

Ten little fingers and ten little toes,
Where are they going?
Nobody knows.

Two little eyes and one little nose,
Where are they going?
Nobody knows.

All dressed up in buttons and bows,
Where are they going?
Nobody knows.

How Many Dogs to Make a Dash?

How many dogs to make a dash?
How many hogs to make a hash?
How many cymbals to make a crash?
How many puddles to make a splash?
How many splashes to make a bath
For Jonathan Jordan Jeffrey Nash?

Welcome Baby, Dear

Welcome, welcome Baby, Dear.
Like a star, you have suddenly come
Out of the always and everywhere
Into our heart's kingdom.

In Disguise

My disguise was nearly perfect.
My hat was pulled way down,
A cape was thrown around my neck,
My face was all a frown.
I sneaked into the kitchen
While she was having tea.
But Mommy said, "Oh, hi there Jack."
How did she know that it was me?

I'd Rather Ride a Chair

Hi Ho! Hi Ho! I'd rather ride a chair.
Hi Ho! Hi Ho! From here to everywhere.
Hi Ho! Hi Ho! I never have a care.
Hi Ho! Hi Ho! If I don't go anywhere.

Blow a bubble.

Blow a bubble,
Watch it grow

Blow a bubble,
Let it go.

Blow a bubble
In the air.

Bubble,
Bubble
Everywhere.

He Wasn't Too Big

He wasn't too big to dance a jig
When they sang "Hey diddle diddle."
But he was too kind to beat the drum
So he just rum-a-tummed on the fiddle.

Buttons

I wonder what
Could be the reason
To put the buttons
Where no one sees 'em?

The Journey

Oh, we're not going anywhere,
Anywhere, anywhere.
But we're going really fast!
And I'll be the first one,
First one, first one,
And the littlest one is last!

Pancakes

Pancakes for you,
Pancakes for me.
Pancakes for two,
Pancakes for three.
Pancakes with syrup
Or gooseberry jam.
Pancakes with bacon
Or pancakes with ham.
They can slapdash them
Or make them with flair.
When people
Make you pancakes,
You just know
That they care.

If I Were a Sailor Man

If I were a sailor man I'd dance a little tune.
If I were a sailor man I'd sail by light of moon.
If I were a sailor man, no matter what they said,
If I were a sailor man, I wouldn't go up to bed!

Dolly and Me

When I'm all alone, just me, me, me,
I can make my dolly some tea, tea, tea.
Then I am as happy as can be, be, be.
If you come and visit, you will see, see, see.

Where are the Girls?

Their mother has called them a dozen times,
There has been no answering sound.
Reagan, McKay, Kelsey Belle and
Delaney are not to be found.
Mom looks into the playroom,
She checks the hall and bath.
She still hears no one crying,
She still hears no one laugh.
Then out back, by the play yard,
Sitting in a line, she finds four solemn faces
In the afternoon sunshine.
She tiptoes back in silence,
No wonder they hadn't heard.
The triplets are teaching Delaney to read,
And they know not a single word!

Have You Hugged Your Doll?

Before you run outside to play
Have you hugged your doll today?
Have you told her "I love you,"
And checked to see how tall she grew,
And made sure that she didn't cry,
And taught her how to wave bye-bye,
And tied her shoes, and combed her hair,
And found her favorite teddy bear?

When I Fall Down

When I fall down and skin my knee,
My mom can kiss it well for me.
She cleans it up, then pats it dry,
And tells me it's all right to cry.

If Every Child

If every little child
Could get a kiss
   good-night
Then I think
   the world
Would finally be
   all right.

Grandmas

"Grandmas are
   the best."
Samantha said.
"They cut the peels
   off apples
And cut the crusts
   off bread."

Meagan's Boat

Her mother's shoes didn't fit at all
When she paraded down the hall.
So dress-up wasn't so much fun,
She couldn't walk, she couldn't run.
Then Meagan found a shoe could float
And my, that made a lovely boat.

Neither of the children made a single sound
Peering in the hole where the rabbit ran down.
Jon took his sister's bonnet and held it like a cup
So they could catch the rabbit when the rabbit came up.
The jolly bluebird chucked from his tree.
He knows that rabbits don't get caught so easily.

Fairy Wings

Whenever the fairies
Wash their wings
And hang them up to dry,
I take out my umbrella
And keep myself quite dry.

I wonder

Sometimes I wonder.
If it were allowed,
How many angels
Could play on a cloud?

Demming Elizabeth

Demming Elizabeth,
Fancy that,
Tried to eat
Her mother's hat.
Got right to
The very crown
Before they made her
Put it down.
"It's just as well,"
I heard her say,
"I didn't like it anyway."

The Smartest Kitty

My kitty plays piano,
She's smart as she can be.
My kitty plays piano
Almost as good as me.

Up and Down

That's the way the world goes,
Up and down, up and down.
Run around the corner twice
You end up back in town.

Salt Their Tails

That hen and duck they go so fast
My running fails to match them.
"Just salt their tails," my Grandma said,
"It never fails to catch them."

A Pig is Perfect

A whale's too big, an ant's too small.
A snake's too short, giraffe's too tall.
A cat can't swim, a fish can't crawl.
A pig is perfect.

A bull's too mean, a cow's too slow.
A mole can't see, a snail won't go.
A bird's too high, a worm's too low.
A pig is perfect.

My Baby Sister

My baby sister doesn't understand
Exactly what it is you should *not* say
When someone tells you that "this is a secret."
This is what she told me yesterday.
"Shh. I saw your birthday present,
And it's hidden in the hall."
Then she whispered even lower
"It's a secret it's a doll."

The Little Artist

My mother is very busy,
My father has gone to work.
My sister is being a bother,
My brother is being a jerk.
So when the day turns out like that,
I paint a picture for my cat.

Playing House

The triplets are playing house.
They each have a rocking chair,
They each have their favorite doll
With which they take great care.
They sing to them and hug them,
And talk about the day,
And tell them the important things
That mommies always say.
"I'll fix you a nice dinner, then when you are fed,
I will read your favorite book and tuck you into bed."

Katie Shall Not

"No, No," said Katie firmly,
Take those crusts away.
I will not, shall not eat them
Though you keep me here all day!
I will not, shall not eat them,
Though you sit me in my chair!
I will not, shall not eat them,
And that I do declare!
I will not, shall not eat them,
And that I tell you plain!
I will not, shall not eat them
Though I never eat again!

The Flower Fairies

I was talking to the flowers
All by myself one day.
Suddenly, the wind came down
And blew the petals all around.
Then, to my complete surprise,
And right before my very eyes,
They turned to fairies in disguise.
I hoped that they would stay and play,
But they just waved and flew away.

Picking Flowers

Delaney and the triplets
Have been in the yard for hours
Picking the yellow dandelions,
It's one of their favorite flowers.
They like the wishing flowers too,
They're the blossoms gone to seed.
They take a breath and make a wish
As they blow the fluff in the breeze.

Kelsey Found a Kitty

Kelsey found a kitty;
It was white and gray.
It was very little,
It didn't get in the way.
It didn't scratch, it didn't bite,
It didn't even howl at night.
It went to the kitchen and caught a rat
You can't ask for a better cat than that!

Once I Had a Friend

Once I had a friend
Who gave me a rose.
He hadn't any shoes
But he had lots of toes.
He hadn't any money
But he had on a hat.
If I ever have another friend
I hope he's just like that.

What Does Delaney Say?

Mommy says, "We're late for school.
Jump in the car, Let's go, let's go."
And then what does Delaney say?
 "Uh oh! Uh oh! Uh oh!"

Daddy says, "Stop that right now,
Our toys and books we do not throw."
And then what does Delaney say?
"Uh oh! Uh oh! Uh oh!"

Mommy says, "Don't touch that fish
It's sure to fall, down it will go."
And then what does Delaney say?
"Uh oh! Uh oh! Uh oh!"

243

In Fairyland

Though it seems strange,
They are the proper size.
So fairyland has now arranged
That fairies fly on flies.

Child Flying Day

In Fairyland, one day a year
Is called Child Flying Day.
The birds fly down,
And then they take
The children up to play.

A Coach and Six

Oh, I'd like to have a coach and six.
I'd crack my whip, and off we'd rumble,
Racing down the streets of town.
Oh, wouldn't my friends all grumble
To see me ride in great estate
As if I were a king?
I'd bow and offer them a ride
Like any normal thing!

Black Currant Jelly

Now maybe you'll think this is terribly silly,
But Kelsey was crazy for black currant jelly.
She'd steal it from the cupboard
When no one was about.
There'd be silence in the kitchen,
And then someone would shout:
"Kelsey's in the jam again."
Whatever shall we do?
She eats it by the spoonful,
And drops it on her shoe.
She grabs it by the fistful,
And glops it on her dress.
Ugh! Her hair is sticky!
Arggh! She's such a mess!
Then Mama grabs
The washcloth,
And Papa grabs
The mop,
And Kelsey starts to cry
As if she'll never stop.
And Grammy says,
 "Poor child, there, there,
We've currant jelly enough to spare."

247

My Conscience

My conscience has been bothering me,
I can't imagine why.
I didn't steal a cookie, I didn't tell a lie.
Do you think he could be mad
That I pinched my little brother?
It was only just a little pinch,
And nobody saw it
Under the cover.

The Haircut

Why ever did that poor, poor child
Cut off her hair like that?
She did not think ahead, oh my!
She looks like some skinned rat.
She said she knew that it was wrong
But it was fun to do it.
Of course she wants her hair back now
So she's asking mom to glue it.

Just Let that Go on By

Reagan says, "McKay's not fair.
She has a doll and she won't share."
Grammy says, "Oh my, Oh my.
Just let that go on by."

Kelsey says "Reagan's not fair,
She put *my* ribbon on *her* bear."
Grammy says, "Oh my, Oh my.
Just let that go on by."

McKay says, "Give me back my book.
Mom, look at what Delaney took."
Grammy says, "Oh my, Oh my.
Just let that go on by."

Little things shouldn't make you mad.
Think of this when you are sad,
Grammy says, "Oh my, Oh my.
Just let that go on by."

Don't Tell Me What to Do

"Don't tell me what to do—
You're not the boss of me."
The little guy meant every word
It was plain as it could be.
It's hard to get that message through
To his much bigger brother,
But it was brave of him to not
Go running to his Mother.

A Little Push

Patiently waiting
There she will sit,
If Delancy Ann
Wants to swing a bit.
She loves to go "high"
Where the air goes woosh.
Won't somebody give her
Just one little push?

Delaney Took a Dishcloth

Delaney took a dishcloth
And got right down to work.
She cleaned the walls,
She cleaned the floor.
She cleaned them once
Then cleaned some more.
She just kept cleaning,
Nothing stopped it
Until she cleaned a plate
And dropped it.

My Daughter Sunday

A flower grows at our house that grows no other place:
A blue-eyed Sunday looking up through freckles on her face,
A pink forget-me-not with blonde hair almost to her knee,
Who, half-way down the walk, runs back for one more kiss from me.
Who droops into a rainy frown, then bubbles up all laugh,
And picks the blossoms off the other flowers on her path.
So sweetly slays them with her love, at six she is not wise
That when you take it for yourself, the flower always dies.

How Beautiful

Do you know how beautiful you are?
Do you know how beautiful you are?
Do you know how beautiful you are?

There Were Two Sisters

There were two sisters who lived in a basket
And never a person knew why.
If you have a question I hope you will ask it,
And if they will tell you, it won't be a lie.

My Friend

I wish my friend would play with me.
Why does she run away from me?
If she comes back I'll share my toys,
And maybe not make so much noise.
And maybe I won't be so mean,
And won't eat most of her ice cream.
And maybe not push her aside
And try to be first on the slide.
And maybe I won't spash the water
In her face like I shouldn't oughter.

Reciprocity

My sister said,
And I think it's true,
That all the flowers
Like us, too!

I know a Boy Named Reese

I know a boy named Reese,
Who in the coldest weather
Will not wear a coat to school.
He will not take a sweater.
"Looks like a storm," his mother says,
"You must take an umbrella."
But what's a little shower of rain
To such a plucky fellow?

The Lie

I told a lie
And everybody's mad.
It popped right out
Before I knew it.
Really, I didn't mean
To do it.
But now
it's done.
Next time
A lie comes on
My tongue,
I'm going to bite it
Right in two,
Like every good child
Ought to do.

Combing Out Tangles

I can't comb out these tangles, I never will be through.
For every one that I comb out, there are three more to do.
Everywhere I touch my head, there is another knot.
How come I have such snarly hair, when I would rather not?
Mommy does it faster, she makes those snarls behave,
And even when it hurts a bit, I know how to be brave.

McKay Likes Pink.

McKay likes pink.
She goes to the closet,
And what do you think?
Does she pick out a blue dress
A green one, or red? A brown one, or purple?
"No, no, no," she said,
And her blue eyes sparkle and twink.
"I want the pink one!
The pink one! The pink one!
I like PINK!"

What Shall We Do?

What shall we do with Elizabeth Sue?
We must watch her every minute.
She opens every pocketbook
So she can see what's in it.
We wonder what is on her mind.
What is it that she thinks she'll find?
She can't be looking for a frog,
A turtle or a bird.
To look for these in someone's purse
Would simply be absurd.
She can't be looking for a snake,
She's too afraid of those.
She can't be looking for a tree,
A tulip, or a rose.
She can't be looking for a horse,
A horse would never fit.
Perhaps she thinks there's candy there
And she will have a bit.
Perhaps she thinks she'll find a pipe,
And then she'll blow a bubble.
But if her mother catches her,
All she will find is trouble.

Take Your Medicine

The little baby elephant won't take his medicine,
No matter how his mama tries her best to get it in.
His little mouth is closed up tight,
He just opens it to yell.
It's very sad because he's sick,
And medicine would make him well.
Tell that baby elephant to swallow it real quick.
That's how you take your medicine
Whenever you are sick.

Nicole's Kitten

My kitten has a long, long name
And she is very pretty.
Her name is Genevieve Sierra Petunia Toto Kitty.
She is five years old, and she is very neat.
Her favorite place
For sleeping
Is on my daddy's feet.

Where are the Keys?

"Where are the keys, Girls?" Mother asked.
"They *were* right by the door,
And now they're gone. What shall we do?
We can't be late once more.
Who took the keys? Let's all look please,
They did not lose themselves."
The triplets looked behind the desk
And on the kitchen shelves.
Then Kelsey called, "I see them!
They're running down the stairs."
And Reagan tried to stop them
With her teddy bears.
McKay called, "Daddy help us!"
And before they disappeared,
He reached and caught them just in time,
And everybody cheered.

I Met the Nicest Mermaid

I met the nicest mermaid yesterday.
She helped me build a castle,
But the waves washed it away.
The mermaid laughed,
And then her long tail swished,
And waves would bring us sea shells,
As many as we wished.
"I'd like to meet your mermaid friend," said Mom.
But when I pointed to the waves,
That nice mermaid was gone!

The Little Digger

First I'm going to dig for gold,
Then I'll dig for treasure.
Then I'll dig the biggest cave
That you could ever measure.
Then I'll dig a tunnel.
Then I'll dig a pit
To capture some wild animal
And make a pet of it.
Then I'll dig a river
To see where it will run.
When I run out of things to dig
Then I'll just dig for fun.

Morgan's Cart

You can ride the fastest train that takes you far from home.
You can sail the smoothest ship upon the ocean foam.
You can drive the biggest truck if you figure how to haul it,
But I just want a little cart that comes when I call it

The Triplets at a Petting Zoo

A little lamb at the petting zoo
Must have wandered off by itself.
The triplets saw that it was lost
And went to get some help.
Reagan said "It's a baby lamb."
But Kelsey said "It's a llama."
"Whatever the poor thing is" said McKay,
"I think it needs its mama."

Just Don't Play With the Dragon

You can play with the kitten, you can play with the cat.
You can play with the buzzards, you can play with the bat.
You can play with the ponies, you can play with the pup.
But just don't play with the dragon,
'Cause the dragon's gonna eat you up!

You can play with the horses, you can play with the dogs.
You can play with the piggies, you can play with the hogs.
You can play with your grandma if you don't interrupt.
But just don't play with the dragon,
'Cause the dragon's gonna eat you up!

You can play with the beetles, you can play with the bugs.
You can play with the froggies, you can play with the slugs.
You can play with the beastie if he asks you to sup.
But just don't play with the dragon,
'Cause the dragon's gonna eat you up!

ALL ABOARD!

The rocker will be the engine,
We'll make the cars out of chairs.
We'll ride around the country,
You'll see how everyone stares
At our faces in the window
As our wonderful train goes by.
Then we'll stop and ring the bell,
"All aboard, all aboard," we'll cry.
And they'll ask, "Where are you going?
To London, to France, to the Fair?"
And we'll say, "Yes, hop on, let's go.
Wherever you want, we'll go there."

My Dog is a Horse

My dog is really a horse.
Sometimes he barks and wags his tail,
But that's not his *real* self.
I'm waiting for him to whinny and neigh,
And when he does, we'll gallop away.

Deane's Lion Poem

"The lions are here,
Over there, by the wall.
They hid in the dark
When I came down the hall.
They crouched underneath
As I climbed into bed.
They can't scare *me*, though,
Those bad lions," he said.
"*Bad* lions never bite me
'Cause *laughing* lions like me."

Is That all There is?

Is that all there is?
Just play in the water, and dig in the sand,
And throw the ball to Elizabeth Ann?
Just swing on my swing, and slide on my slide,
And look for the little shells after the tide?

Dragon Hill

Whenever I go to Dragon Hill
I take along some porridge.
I share it with the dragons
So they don't use me for forage.

They Sing So Sweetly

The birds sing so sweetly I think Heaven sent them.
I don't think somebody could ever invent them.

Holloween Costumes

We're dressing up for Halloween.
We'll trick or treat both near and far.
And if you'll tell me who *I* am,
I'll tell you who I think *you* are.

Jack-O-Lantern

Jack-o-lantern, Jack-o-lantern
Home with me you go.
I'll put you in the window
For a Halloween hello,
For you won't scare the little goblins
With your friendly candle glow.

Trick or Treat

Trick or treat! Trick or treat!
Our costumes now are all complete,
And we are coming down your street.
Won't you give us something sweet?
Trick or treat! Trick or treat!

Ayla, the Picky Dresser

Ayla dresses just in blue,
Or pink, or white, but that's the limit,
Not a green dress, she's won't get in it.
And nothing scratchy, and nothing silly,
And nothing stiff, and nothing frilly.
And not a sweater, for she can't bear it,
And she will never, never wear it!

I Hate It When I Don't Get What I Want

I say "Yes," but they say "No." I want to stay, they want to go.
So I begin complaining, and they commence to shout.
Then they commence to fuss, and I begin to pout.
But what else can I do?
I hate it when I don't get what I want!
Oh, don't you hate it, too?

"Don't play in the water, child,
Or you might drown.
You can only sail your boat
If your boat's on solid ground."
But that's not what I want to do.
Who can stand to sail the sand
Who's sailed the ocean blue?
I hate it when I can't do what I want.
Oh, don't you hate it, too?

Call the King's horses and all the King's men,
Harmony's helping her mother again.
She's watered the plant, and the floor, and her dress.
She's made such a terrible, horrible mess.
The more she helped the worse it grew.
Do things like that ever happen to you?
Oh, don't you hate it, too?

The Snow Fairies

Have you ever seen snow fairies fly?
They live in clouds, you know.
And when they shake their pillows out,
The next day we have snow

The Fairy Queen

When the Fairy Queen must take a trip,
On wings of gold she flies,
And hails the nearest rainbow
For her fleet of butterflies.

Let's Pretend

Let's pretend we're on an island,
Oh, I know, it's just our yard.
But play like we've been shipwrecked,
Come on, it's not that hard.
We'll wave as all the boats go by
And maybe when they see us,
They'll come in for a rescue,
Thinking they will free us.
Then we can pick some flowers
And give them to the crew,
And say, "Thank you" to the captain,
"That was very nice of you."

Peregrine is Eight

Peregrine is eight years old.
He's brave and smart and quick and bold.
He plays piano as good as can be,
Oh, don't you wish that you were he?

Hide and Seek

When Peregrine plays hide and seek,
It's not for the mild and it's not for the meek.
They all run scared,
And never look behind them,
For Peregrine will never fail to find them.

Teddy's Turn

My teddy bear complained
(It was hard to disagree)
That I bounced him down the bannister
And tossed him in a tree.
He says I'd learn a lesson
And a fair thing it would be
If one day I couldn't play with him
And he, instead, could play with me.

The Mystery

We asked the bluebirds if they knew it,
Offered them seeds, and day-old suet.
"We just don't know," they begged our pardon,
"Why the triplets are crying in the garden.
McKay always cries when Kelsey's crying.
When Reagan cries, Kelsey cries too.
But what's the matter with Reagan?
We haven't a single clue!"

The Mouse

"Eeek!" said Amanda. "Squeak!" said the mouse.
 "Out," said Amanda, "out of my house!
It's not that you scared me, or gave me a fright.
But to sneak in my pantry is just not polite."

Little Miss Bunchen

Little Miss Bunchen
Sat down for luncheon,
Eating her burger with cheese.
Then came a grasshopper
To munch on her Whopper
With nary a "Thank you" or "Please."

Growing Tall

They tell me I am growing tall.
It is so very strange.
I'm always looking at myself,
I never see me change.
No, not the teensist eensist bit,
Though I stand at the mirror and watch.
If I turn on the light in the dark of the night,
I'm always the same; exactly, quite.
So what I really want to know,
Tell me please, when do I grow?

When Reagan Invites You

When Reagan invites you for tea,
She knows just what to do.
She feeds you cake and cookies,
Sugar and marmalade too.
I always mind my manners,
And remember to say, "Please,"
And "Thank you, dearest Reagan,"
And give her a hug and a squeeze.

Ray's Favorite Poem

Two diving ducklings in a row
Raced the river to and fro.
The slow one sighed, "Alas, alacker,
Would I were the quicker quacker."

Just Be Yourself

Whether you are top drawer,
Or plain bottom shelf,
You'll always be happy
If you just be yourself!

McKay

She cheers me up no matter what bugs me.
She has blue eyes and often shrugs me.
When I start to leave, she runs and tugs me,
And McKay is always the first who hugs me.

Reagan

Reagan, Shaygan, Shigon, Shu
Will read you a book if you ask her to.
She's such a good reader, I've heard it said,
That she must have a million words in her head.

When Nobody Loves Me

My friend is being mean today
She pinches me and shoves me.
But I can play all my myself
When nobody loves me!

I Watch the Moon

I love to watch the silvery moon
Sail in its silent sea.
It came by my window again tonight
And stopped right over the maple tree.
I watch the moon, I watch the moon
And the moon watches over me.

Index of Titles